CLASS IN AMERICA

BEING POOR
IN AMERICA

BY DUCHESS HARRIS, JD, PHD
WITH NEL YOMTOV

Essential Library

An Imprint of Abdo Publishing | abdopublishing.com

ABDOPUBLISHING.COM

Published by Abdo Publishing, a division of ABDO, PO Box 398166, Minneapolis, Minnesota 55439.
Copyright © 2019 by Abdo Consulting Group, Inc. International copyrights reserved in all countries.
No part of this book may be reproduced in any form without written permission from the publisher.
Essential Library™ is a trademark and logo of Abdo Publishing.

Printed in the United States of America, North Mankato, Minnesota
042018
092018

**THIS BOOK CONTAINS
RECYCLED MATERIALS**

Cover Photo: Lost + Taken
Interior Photos: iStockphoto, 5, 17, 19, 24–25, 55, 63, 64, 66, 68, 77, 79, 85; Denis Tangney Jr./
iStockphoto, 7, 39; Red Line Editorial, 9, 20, 41, 56, 88; Juan Monino/iStockphoto, 11; WA/AP Images,
14; David McNew/Getty Images News/Getty Images, 29; Everett Collection Historical/Alamy, 31, 35;
Schulmann-Sachs/picture-alliance/dpa/AP Images, 33; Yacob Chuk/iStockphoto, 44; Shutterstock
Images, 47; Lauri Lyons/Photonica World/Getty Images, 51; William F. Campbell/The LIFE Images
Collection/Getty Images, 61; Brandy Taylor/iStockphoto, 75; Steve Debenport/iStockphoto, 80, 97; J.
Scott Applewhite/AP Images, 93; Ron Sachs/picture-alliance/dpa/AP Images, 95

Editor: Kari Cornell
Series Designer: Becky Daum

LIBRARY OF CONGRESS CONTROL NUMBER: 2017961135

PUBLISHER'S CATALOGING-IN-PUBLICATION DATA

Names: Harris, Duchess, author. | Yomtov, Nel, author.
Title: Being poor in America / by Duchess Harris and Nel Yomtov.
Description: Minneapolis, Minnesota : Abdo Publishing, 2019. | Series: Class in America | Includes
      online resources and index.
Identifiers: ISBN 9781532114045 (lib.bdg.) | ISBN 9781532153877 (ebook)
Subjects: LCSH: Poverty--United States--Juvenile literature. | Poor--Services for--United States--
      Juvenile literature. | Poor families--United States--Juvenile literature. | Poor--Medical
      care--United States--Juvenile literature. | Social classes--United States--History--
      Juvenile literature.
Classification: DDC 301.451--dc23

CONTENTS

ONE

THE AMERICAN WAY
OF POVERTY

The doctor told Rachel Andrews she had cancer. The news hit the 42-year-old mother of three children like a bolt of lightning. The cancer was in her intestine. But there was reason for hope: the doctor said an operation would completely remove the cancer and have her in good health.

Andrews smiled weakly, nodding her head. She had no choice. She would have the operation that would save her life. Andrews took a temporary leave of absence from her job as a secretary and bookkeeper. While she was hospitalized, her husband and children would continue living in the same house in New York City where they had lived for seven years. Life for her and her family would return to normal once she fully recovered.

A person who is unable to work due to illness may have no money to pay for housing. Some families may lose their homes as a result.

Andrews underwent not one, but three operations to remove the stubborn cancer. She was unable to return to work. During her time in the hospital, things at home changed dramatically. Her husband of 13 years began having troubles of his own. He began drinking heavily and became aggressive and destructive around the house and with the children.

Trying to maintain her own health and well-being, Andrews had no strength to help her husband. She took her children— two daughters and one son—and left their home. At first, she rented a small apartment with her savings. But because she had taken a leave from work, Andrews had no money coming in. Finally, she had to give up the place.

Andrews felt embarrassed and defeated. But she was also desperate. She had no choice but to apply for government assistance.

For a week, during the daytime and early evening, Andrews and the children waited in a government welfare office to be helped. The children did not attend school. At night, the family got a few hours of sleep in an emergency assistance unit (EAU) for homeless people that was run by the city. The shelter was dirty and unsafe. The only food provided for the family was peanut butter and jelly or cheese sandwiches.

Finally, Andrews and her three children were sent by the city to live in a hotel that housed other homeless families.

The room was in shambles. There was no running water. Fearing for her children's health and safety, Andrews returned to the government office to plead for a better place to stay. She was told that nothing could be done, and she was sent back to the EAU—where she and the children spent the next month.

Then came more bad news. Andrews's 14-year-old daughter became ill. She had surgery to remove a tumor on her kidney. The doctor told Andrews that the teen could not sit upright in the government welfare office. For the next three days, the family, armed with the doctor's letter, went to the welfare office. Andrews hoped the letter would convince the welfare workers to find her family an apartment so her daughter would not have to wait in the offices. Each day, however, the family was sent back to the EAU.

Finally, after 45 days of homelessness, the Andrews were sent to another city-run hotel. Conditions were a little better than the first hotel, but her new room was robbed four times. Andrews was weary, fearful, and nearly without hope. Her former boss wanted her back, but if she returned to work, she would lose her hotel room and her other government benefits, such as food stamps.

Andrews was in a tough situation. She could not pay rent and care for her children on her secretary's salary. The food stamps she received were barely enough to feed herself and the kids. Many days, Andrews ate only one meal, saving the rest

US POVERTY RATE[2]

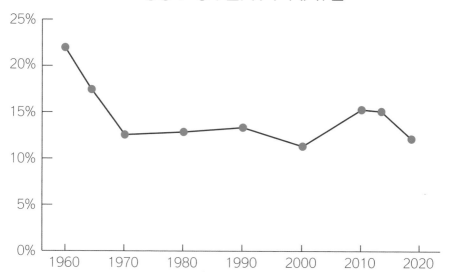

The War on Poverty, introduced in the 1960s, was effective in reducing the number of people living in poverty in the United States.

so the children could eat more often. There was little money, if any, for new clothing. Visiting a museum or going to the movies was impossible. The family's life was a daily struggle, and worse, Andrews was terrified that her children would never escape life in poverty.

The Andrews family is not alone. Tens of millions of people in the United States—one of the wealthiest nations on Earth—live in poverty. Each day, these people live the grim reality of being poor in America.

WHAT IS POVERTY?

Poverty is described in the dictionary as "the state of being poor; the lack of the means of providing material needs or comforts."[1] Yet how is the "state of being poor" determined? Poverty is measured in many ways, each focusing on different economic and social conditions. The United States generally relies on what is known as an absolute measure of poverty, which is related to the amount of money required to meet basic human needs such as food, clothing, and shelter.

HOW POVERTY AFFECTS THE US ECONOMY

Poverty rates in America are closely related to the overall health of the nation's economy. Researchers have discovered that the economic costs of poverty are staggering. Childhood poverty alone costs the US economy more than $500 billion each year in higher health-care costs, lost productivity, and lower earnings. Poverty is often accompanied by higher crime rates, which results in higher spending by law enforcement agencies and criminal courts.

Every year, the federal government establishes new poverty thresholds, or "poverty lines," for individuals and families. An individual or family with annual income less than the threshold is considered to be living in poverty.[3] For example, in 2016, the poverty threshold for one person was $12,228 per year; for two, the threshold was $15,569. Higher thresholds are established for families with children. The threshold for a family of five people was $29,111; for nine people or more,

initiative to eliminate poverty in the United States. Since then, the United States has spent more than $22 trillion on government welfare programs—more than three times the amount spent on all wars in the nation's history.[10]

And yet poverty in the United States persists. Its rate ebbs and flows over time, but poverty remains a plague on the nation. Strong efforts continue to be made in the fight against poverty, and many anti-poverty initiatives have worked. Social Security, Medicaid, and food stamps, for example, have relieved the financial burdens of millions of Americans and helped them in times of need. The Center on Budget and Policy Priorities, a nonpartisan policy and research organization, claims that poverty rates would be double without these programs. Most people would agree the fight against poverty must be continued. The question is: can America win the war?

DISCUSSION STARTERS

- How would you define poverty? What do you think causes it?

- Do you think federal, state, and local governments should be responsible for providing welfare assistance? Why or why not?

- Do you believe poverty can be eliminated in the United States? Explain your thoughts.

TWO

THE CAUSES AND
FACTORS OF
POVERTY

P overty is a complex issue. The World Bank Organization, an international group of banks that lend money to developing nations, states, "Poverty is hunger. Poverty is lack of shelter. . . . Poverty is not having access to school and not knowing how to read. Poverty is not having a job, is fear for the future, living one day at a time."[1]

People living in poverty lack many material things, but they also lack political power—the ability to change or reform some economic aspect of American society, including those conditions that keep alive their own personal cycle of generational poverty.

There is no single cause of poverty. The conditions and factors that result in poverty vary from individual to individual.

The poorest Americans live one paycheck away from not having enough money to buy food or pay rent.

Nor is poverty a static, unchanging circumstance. Older adults are less poor than they were 40 years ago, and unlike in the past, today children make up the poorest age group. Poverty in the suburbs has dramatically risen. In fact, poverty in the suburbs is growing at a rate higher than urban poverty. The causes of impoverishment are at the heart of most discussions about poverty and the poor.

IS IMMIGRATION A FACTOR?

The number of immigrants living in the United States has increased from 9.6 million people in 1970 to more than 43 million in 2017.[2] Some people believe immigration increases poverty in the United States. They argue that the large number of unskilled immigrant laborers forces US-born workers out of the job market. This allows employers to pay lower wages, thereby putting less money in people's pockets and increasing the level of poverty in the country. Others assert that the influx of unskilled immigrants encourages US citizens to gain higher skills and education. In turn, this stimulates overall economic growth in the United States.

UNEMPLOYMENT AND STAGNANT WAGES

A lack of adequately paying jobs is a key cause of America's high rates of poverty. There are not enough living wage jobs to support all US households. Many people live in poverty because they cannot find a decent-paying job or any job at all.

Long-term unemployment affects both skilled and unskilled workers. Low-skilled workers are especially vulnerable during

times of high unemployment in the country, such as the global financial crisis that began in 2007. Yet it's not uncommon for out-of-work high-skilled workers, such as engineers and financial professionals, to be unemployed for long periods. In April 2017, 1.6 million Americans had been out of work for six months or more. Approximately 1 million had been without jobs for a year.[3]

The cost of renting an apartment varies from state to state. This map indicates how much a household needed to make per hour to afford a two-bedroom apartment in 2017.

THE HOURLY WAGE PEOPLE NEED TO RENT A TWO-BEDROOM APARTMENT[4]

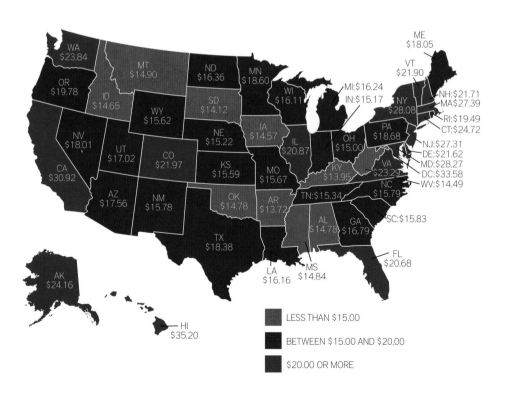

ME $18.05
WA $23.84
VT $21.90
MT $14.90
ND $16.36
MN $18.60
OR $19.78
ID $14.65
WI $16.11
MI:$16.24
NH:$21.71
MA$27.39
NY $28.08
IN:$15.17
SD $14.12
WY $15.62
RI:$19.49
CT:$24.72
NV $18.01
NE $15.22
IA $14.57
PA $18.68
UT $17.02
CO $21.97
IL $20.87
OH $15.00
NJ:$27.31
DE:$21.62
CA $30.92
KS $15.59
MO $15.67
KY $13.95
VA $23.29
MD:$28.27
DC:$33.58
WV:$14.49
AZ $17.56
NM $15.78
OK $14.78
AR $13.72
TN:$15.34
NC $15.79
AL $14.78
GA $16.79
SC:$15.83
TX $18.38
FL $20.68
AK $24.16
LA $16.16
MS $14.84
HI $35.20

LESS THAN $15.00
BETWEEN $15.00 AND $20.00
$20.00 OR MORE

In many cases, the longer an individual is unemployed, the more difficult it becomes for him or her to find a job.

Since the 1980s, the hourly wages of the majority of American minimum wage workers have stagnated and not kept pace with inflation. In 1938, the US government set the minimum wage at $0.25 per hour. The goal was to ensure that no employee fell below a certain wage rate. Since then, that rate has been raised 22 times. But because the minimum wage is not determined by inflation rates, its buying power has actually decreased through the years. In 1968, the minimum wage was $1.60, which was equivalent to $11.40 in 2017.[5]

In comparison, the minimum wage in January 2018 was $7.25 an hour. If an individual earns $7.25 per hour working a full-time job (35 hours per week in a 52-week period, totaling 1,820 hours per year), he or she would earn a total of $13,195, which is less than $1,000 above the national poverty threshold.[6]

THE GLOBAL FINANCIAL CRISIS AND POVERTY

The financial crisis of 2007–2008 was one of the world's worst financial disasters since the Great Depression of the 1930s. Stock markets plummeted around the world. Dozens of banks, insurance companies, and other financial institutions went bankrupt. The American automobile industry nearly collapsed. As unemployment skyrocketed, many working Americans living in poverty lost their jobs. An estimated 7.5 million to 10 million people were pushed into poverty. The number of Americans who applied for government assistance increased significantly.

IS POVERTY A SERIOUS PROBLEM?

Some experts believe that most people defined by the US government as living in poverty enjoy a comfortable standard of living. Robert Rector, a leading politically conservative researcher and writer on poverty and welfare programs, claims few of those people are "actually poor." Rector concedes "real hardship does exist," but he says government surveys support his claim. According to Rector, the surveys show the typical "poor" American has satellite or cable television and owns two TVs. Nearly three-quarters of poor households own a car, and approximately one-third own two or more cars. Nearly 40 percent of the American poor own their own homes; on average they have a three-bedroom house. Rector attributes much of the poverty in the United States to "low levels of parental work, on average, sixteen hours for the typical poor family with children."[8] However, although some Americans living in poverty have a more comfortable standard of living than those who are impoverished in poor nations, poverty in the United States is very real. The United States has one of the highest rates of poverty and child poverty among developed nations. Forty-one million Americans struggle with hunger daily. Recent data illustrates the serious nature of poverty in America. In the book *$2.00 a Day: Living on Almost Nothing in America*, researchers Kathryn Edin and Luke Shaefer report that 1.5 million American households, including 3 million children, live on $2.00 per person, per day.[9]

Many people argue that increasing the minimum wage would help reduce poverty. According to a 2014 Congressional Budget Office report, increasing the minimum wage to $9.00 would lift 300,000 Americans out of poverty, and an increase to $10.10 would lift 900,000 people out of poverty.[7] Supporters claim an increase in the federal minimum wage would reduce government welfare spending and reduce income inequality. Opponents of an increase argue that employers would have to lay off workers to afford the increase, thus raising unemployment levels nationwide. The US Congress has the sole power to set minimum wage levels.

RACE AND ETHNICITY

Race and ethnicity are major issues in the discussion of poverty and the poor. Overall, in the United States, minority groups are worse off than whites, according to several economic measurements. In 2016, blacks and Hispanics had the nation's highest rates of poverty at 22 percent and 19.4 percent, respectively. In some states, the poverty rates of blacks are significantly higher than the rates of poverty among whites. In Minnesota, blacks had a poverty rate of 38 percent, whereas 7 percent of whites lived in poverty. Poverty rates in the District of Columbia were 27 percent for black Americans and 6 percent for white Americans. In Maine, the poverty rate of blacks was nearly eight times the rate of whites, 87 percent compared with 11 percent.[10]

Regarding earnings, the median household income for blacks in 2016 was $39,490; for Hispanics, it was $47,675. Comparatively, the median household income for whites was $65,041. Median income is the income level in the middle of ranked incomes. For example, if a neighborhood has five households with incomes of $15,000, $20,000, $30,000, $52,000, and $95,000, the median household income of that area is the middle figure, $30,000.

Success in elementary school increases the likelihood that children will graduate from high school and go on to college.

Historically, minorities in the United States have had less access to jobs and education than whites. Therefore, they are more likely to have lower levels of education, employment, and wages—all of which are linked to higher poverty rates. Race also figures into the availability of assistance for the poor. The National Poverty Center at the University of Michigan, which researches poverty, reports that residents of predominantly black or Hispanic neighborhoods have access to half as many social services as those in predominantly white neighborhoods.

EDUCATION

The relationship between education and family income shows that heads of households with more education earn more money. In 2016, the median household income of a family headed by someone who dropped out of high school was $28,400. Families headed by an individual with a bachelor's degree had a median household income of $93,000, a difference of $64,600.[11]

Underscoring the differences in earnings between dropouts and degree holders is the high school dropout rate among low-income families. In 2015, the high school dropout rate among persons age 16 to 24 was much higher in low-income families (9.9 percent) as compared with that of high-income families (2.4 percent).[12]

In addition, inequality in educational achievement is as stark as income inequality itself. In 2014, 80 percent of 18- to 24-year-olds from families earning more than $116,466 annually were enrolled in colleges or universities, compared with only 45 percent from families earning less than $34,933.[13]

FAMILY STRUCTURE

Changes in family structure, especially the shift to a higher percentage of single-parent households, also contribute to higher rates of poverty. Although the overall divorce rate in the United States has fallen, divorce among the poor and low-income families has remained roughly consistent. About 17 percent of lower-income couples get divorced, approximately what their divorce rate was in the 1980s. Couples argue about money more than any other issue. In addition, childbearing by unwed mothers usually results in children growing up in single-parent households. Approximately one-half of single parents are poor, which means their children grow up in poverty as well. Children of unmarried mothers tend to attain low levels of education and are more likely to have children outside of marriage themselves.

Many factors contribute to poverty in the United States, including a lack of adequately paying jobs, stagnant wages, race, education, and family structure. For decades, the US government has been looking for solutions to end poverty.

DISCUSSION STARTERS

- Some people claim laziness and an unwillingness to work is the main cause of poverty. What do you think?

- What advantages, if any, do the wealthy in America have? Describe the economic, political, and social benefits of having wealth.

- Do you know anyone who was affected by the global financial crisis of 2007–2008? Has a friend or member of your family ever lost a job? Describe how you might feel if you were laid off from your job.

WEALTH INEQUALITY IN
THE UNITED STATES

The United States has one of the highest standards of living in the world, with a 2016 median household income of $59,039.[14] Yet the wealth is not shared equally among all Americans. There are more families living in poverty today than ever before. The reason is wealth inequality. The rich are getting richer, and the poor are getting poorer. Evidence indicates that in 2017, one percent of the American population held nearly 39 percent of the wealth—up from 34 percent only ten years earlier. In 2007, the bottom 90 percent of lower-income families held nearly 29 percent of the nation's wealth. In 2017, the figure declined to approximately 23 percent.[15]

Why does the gap between the rich and the poor exist—and why is it widening? Some experts attribute the disparity to the same causes of poverty itself: low wages, less access to education, and class, race, and gender discrimination. The growth of technology—especially machinery that can do the work of people—eliminates many low-skilled jobs. In addition, people who already hold wealth can invest it to create more wealth.

Some people believe the concentration of wealth in the hands of a few has severe political consequences. "We're facing a vicious cycle in which more and more of the nation's resources are going to a smaller and smaller sliver of people at the top who, in turn, are exercising more and more political power over how the economy is organized, which gives them even more resources," said Robert Reich, economist and former US secretary of labor.[16]

Robert Reich has looked for ways to shrink inequality.

THREE

AMERICA'S WAR
ON POVERTY

T he post–World War II (1939–1945) years of the 1950s were a time of economic prosperity in the United States. Jobs were plentiful. The housing industry thrived, providing new homes for the millions of US soldiers returning to civilian life. Shiny new automobiles rolled off the production lines in record numbers. Manufacturers of new products such as televisions and modern appliances were barely able to keep up with consumer demand. The nation was at peace and the future was bright. But not for all Americans.

AN EYE-OPENING WORK

In 1962, political activist Michael Harrington wrote *The Other America: Poverty in the United States*—an explosive, influential

While new homes were being built during the postwar economic boom, apartments like this one in New York City's Harlem neighborhood remained abandoned and in disrepair.

book that revealed the lives of the American poor from rural Appalachia to inner cities. Harrington's work was among the first attempts to reveal the enormous divide between the haves and the have-nots in the United States. He wrote:

Tens of millions of Americans are, at this very moment, maimed in body and spirit, existing at levels beneath those necessary for human decency. If these people are not starving, they are hungry, and sometimes fat with hunger, for that is what cheap foods do. They are without adequate housing and education and medical care.[1]

POVERTY AND EDUCATION

In April 1965, Congress passed the Elementary and Secondary Education Act, guaranteeing federal-government funding to aid schools in low-income communities. The funds were used to create preschool programs, purchase textbooks, and fund educational research. In May 1965, Johnson created Head Start, a nationwide program to break the cycle of poverty by addressing the educational, emotional, nutritional, and health needs of disadvantaged preschool children. The Upward Bound program was instituted to help low-income students and those in rural areas to attend college.

Harrington described these Americans as the "invisible poor." He wrote, "The other America, the America of poverty is hidden today. . . . Its millions are socially invisible to the rest of us. . . . The poor are increasingly slipping out of the very experience and consciousness of the nation."[2]

The Other America had a powerful, dramatic effect on American society. It made

President Lyndon B. Johnson wanted to make the United States a fairer society for everyone, regardless of income.

poverty in the United States visible and changed the way many Americans thought about the poor.

THE WAR ON POVERTY

On January 8, 1964, President Johnson declared an "unconditional war on poverty" in his first State of the Union address. "Unfortunately," he said, "many Americans live on the outskirts of hope—some because of their poverty, and some because of their color, and all too many because of both. Our task is to help replace their despair with opportunity." Johnson concluded his brief address by asking Congress and the country to join him in "working for a nation that is free from want."[3]

In May 1964, Johnson outlined what he called his Great Society plan during a commencement address at the University of Michigan at Ann Arbor. "The Great Society rests on abundance and liberty for all. It demands an end to poverty and racial injustice," said Johnson.[4]

Johnson's stirring remarks quickly translated into scores of new laws and the creation of dozens of new federal programs and agencies. Johnson's War on Poverty became the centerpiece of his Great Society and one of the largest and most far-reaching reform plans in US history.

PROGRAMS FOR THE POOR

The cornerstone of the War on Poverty was the Economic Opportunity Act of 1964, legislation that created and funded a variety of anti-poverty programs to help the poor develop job skills, improve their education, and find employment. A program called the Job Corps was created to provide education and training that could help people find decent-paying careers. State and local governments were also empowered to create work-training programs. A Community Action Program was instituted to have local

TITLE I

In 1965, President Johnson signed legislation that included Title I. The purpose of Title I is to assist low-income families whose children attend high-poverty schools. Each year, it provides $14 billion to schools with large populations of low-income students. The funds are used for a variety of purposes, including instruction, counseling, curriculum improvement, and hiring additional teachers and other staff. Some of the programs funded by Title I are intended for students at risk of poor educational achievement. In addition to kids in high-poverty schools, these include children with disabilities, Native American children, and children learning English as a second language.

President Johnson signed the Economic Opportunity Act on August 20, 1964.

neighborhood organizations fight poverty in their own communities. These organizations supplied social services to low-income residents.

The Economic Opportunity Act also created the OEO to coordinate Johnson's anti-poverty programs. As the months passed, the OEO continued to create work-oriented programs to alleviate poverty in America. In 1965, Volunteers in Service to America (VISTA) was founded. After receiving training in North Carolina, VISTA volunteers—mostly men and women age 18 to 21—were sent to work with poverty-stricken people throughout the United States. VISTA established day care centers and helped bring medical care to the sick and needy. The Neighborhood Youth Corps taught job skills and gave employment to young men and women still in school or who had dropped out.

MARTIN LUTHER KING JR. AND THE WAR ON POVERTY

Civil rights activist Rev. Dr. Martin Luther King Jr. was an outspoken critic of President Johnson's War on Poverty. Dr. King was dismayed that the War on Poverty was not being waged with as much energy and intensity as the Vietnam War (1955–1975). In December 1967, believing the War on Poverty was a failure, Dr. King organized the Poor People's Campaign. The campaign was a multiracial effort to correct the perceived shortcomings of the War on Poverty. Dr. King proposed to bring poor people from across the nation to Washington, DC, to demand better education, better employment opportunities, and better housing. Dr. King was assassinated several weeks before the Poor People's Campaign marched on Washington, but the event went ahead as planned. Ultimately, the campaign resulted in only modest changes, including expansion of food stamps and the introduction of Head Start programs in several locations.

NUTRITION AND HEALTH CARE

As the War on Poverty tackled unemployment and education, it also turned to other issues associated with poverty: nutrition and health care. The Food Stamp Act of August 1964 was implemented to prevent hunger and provide nutrition to low-income households. State welfare offices provided people with stamps they could exchange for food at grocery stores. By April 1965, approximately 500,000 people were enrolled in the program; by the end of the decade, approximately 3 million Americans received food stamps.

The Social Security Act Amendments, adopted in July 1965, expanded the benefits of Social Security, a program created in the 1930s. The amendments established Medicare, a program to provide health insurance for retirees, and Medicaid, a program to provide health-care benefits for low-income individuals and families.

President Johnson's efforts to end poverty in America were part of his administration's campaign for human rights. Johnson and his supporters believed that the legislation symbolized the principles of democracy, equal opportunity, and social and economic justice for all Americans. Rather than making people more dependent on government—as critics of the War on Poverty claimed—President Johnson's stated goal was to help those who were unable to help themselves.

DISCUSSION STARTERS

- In 1988, President Ronald Reagan declared, "In the sixties we waged a war on poverty, and poverty won." Do you agree with President Reagan? Explain your answer.

- Can recipients of federal assistance programs become too dependent on the government to meet basic needs? Does government aid diminish an individual's initiative to work?

- Taxpayer dollars fund government assistance programs. Do you think working Americans should pay to support programs for the poor? Why or why not?

FOUR

URBAN
POVERTY

The world's population is becoming increasingly urban. In 2016, nearly 55 percent of the world's population lived in cities.[1] In the United States, cities are home to nearly 63 percent of the total population.[2] According to the Brookings Institution, a research group based in Washington, DC, the poverty rate for cities with more than 1 million residents was 13 percent in 2016. In smaller urban areas with fewer than 200,000 residents, the rate was 17 percent.[3]

THE INNER CITY

The appeal of urban areas is strong. Historically, cities promise more jobs and better living standards. Health care and education in cities are generally of higher quality than in rural areas. More

Housing in poor neighborhoods can be run down or completely uninhabitable.

efficient transportation options and a vibrant cultural scene also make cities appealing.

These qualities of city life attract many poor people from rural areas as well as immigrants and refugees from abroad. Many of these new arrivals, however, discover they can land only low-paying, unskilled jobs. The higher average cost of living in large cities adds further financial burdens to these workers.

Inner cities are also home to high proportions of African Americans, Hispanics, and members of other racial minorities who on average earn lower levels of income. Some experts believe conditions in the inner city greatly hamper these individuals' struggle to escape poverty. Harvard University professor William Julius Wilson, author of *The Truly Disadvantaged*, says some black youth in inner cities are in danger of becoming permanently poor because of

THE POOREST CITIES IN THE UNITED STATES[4]

The US Census Bureau's 2016 American Community Survey, released in September 2017, listed the wealthiest and poorest American cities based on median household income. According to the survey, the ten poorest cities with at least 65,000 people were:

CITY	MEDIAN HOUSEHOLD INCOME
READING, PA	$25,865
FLINT, MI	$25,896
CAMDEN, NJ	$26,738
YOUNGSTOWN, OH	$26,789
CLEVELAND, OH	$27,551
DETROIT, MI	$28,099
DAYTON, OH	$28,894
GARY, IN	$29,522
HIALEAH, FL	$30,495
NEWARK, NJ	$31,100

the "poor educational training that so many black youngsters receive in the public schools and their high school drop-out rates."[5]

CRIME

The inner-city poor face a complex set of challenges generally not experienced in rural areas. Violence and crime are frequent occurrences in the inner city. A study by the US Department of Justice in 2014 showed that individuals in poor households were twice as likely to be the victims of violent crimes as individuals in high-income households.

Inner-city violence affects young and old alike. "You've got to protect yourself because you never know if someone is going to be shooting at you or hit you with a car or something," said one 15-year-old teen living in North Lawndale, a neighborhood in western Chicago, Illinois. In 2016, there were more than 280 shootings and more than 30 murders in North Lawndale. Nearly half of the area's 40,000 residents live in poverty. "Sometimes people just think you have money, and it can cost you your life. I have to look at that person like he's trying to hurt me or take what I've got," the young man added.[6]

SHORTAGES OF AFFORDABLE HOUSING

According to the National Low Income Housing Coalition (NLIHC), an organization that works to assure low-income families in the United States have affordable and decent homes, there is a nationwide shortage of affordable houses for low-income families. The NLIHC reports that the United States has a shortage of 7.4 million affordable rental homes available to extremely low-income households.[7] This means that there are approximately 35 affordable homes for every 100 extremely low-income households in the country.

Poor families that find adequate housing, however, may still face grave financial hardship. The standard definition of affordable housing is a residence on which a household spends no more than 30 percent of its income. The NLIHC determined that 71 percent of extremely low-income households spend more than one-half of their income on rent and utilities, such as electricity and gas. These families are called severe cost-burden households because such a significant portion of

LONG-TERM WELFARE AND POVERTY

In her 1997 book, *It Takes a Nation: A New Agenda for Fighting Poverty*, former US secretary of commerce Rebecca Blank wrote there are two types of poor people. The first are those who have a short spell of poverty and recover. The second are those who live in long-term poverty, year after year. Studies show that long-term poverty in the United States is overwhelmingly concentrated in large cities. "Many of these families [on welfare for four years or more] are working, but their earnings are so low they remain eligible for some cash assistance," said Margy Waller, former advisor on welfare to President Bill Clinton. "Others have not been able to find a job and are likely to face barriers to work."[8]

the family income must be committed toward housing. This leaves fewer dollars for other family basics, such as food, clothing, and medical care.

The shortage of affordable housing is the leading cause of homelessness, according to the National Law Center on Homelessness and Poverty, a legal organization that aims to prevent and end homelessness. "Often [severe cost-burden households] are just one paycheck or rent payment away from being homeless," said Bob Palmer, policy director of Housing Action Illinois, a group formed to protect and expand affordable housing throughout the state. "It's very disturbing that people have to be in this situation."[9]

The affordability of housing depends not only on family or individual income but also on geographic location. For example, the average cost of housing in Omaha, Nebraska, is 74 percent less than the average cost of housing in San Francisco, California. The comparable salary of an individual earning $50,000 in San Francisco would be approximately $25,500 in Omaha.[10]

SEGREGATION

Racial segregation also plays a role in urban poverty. Despite the drop in the levels of racial segregation in US cities since the 1970s, the separation of whites and minorities is still prevalent. In 2015, the average white resident in a metropolitan area lived in a neighborhood that was 72 percent white.[11] Some experts believe

THE WORKING POOR

The US Bureau of Labor Statistics (BLS) defines the "working poor" as people who spend at least 27 consecutive weeks working or looking for work but whose incomes still fall below the official poverty level for their individual or family threshold. In 2015, 8.6 million Americans were among the working poor.[12] Recent studies show that women are more likely than men to be among the working poor. Blacks and Hispanics are more than twice as likely as whites and Asians to be among the working poor. Individuals with less than a high school diploma have the highest working-poor rate.

The BLS cites several major challenges facing the working poor. The working poor lack higher education and hold the lowest-paying, most unstable jobs. One-third of the working poor have health problems that limit their ability to work. The working poor are also more likely to be in one-parent households. Only 30 percent of the working poor live in married-couple families. "An inconvenience to an affluent family—minor car trouble, a brief illness, disrupted child care—is a crisis for them [the working poor]," writes David Shipler in *The Working Poor: Invisible in America*. "Even when the economy is robust, many wander through a borderland of struggle, never getting far from where they started."[13]

racial segregation concentrates poverty to a small number of minority neighborhoods.

Minorities have historically been discriminated against in the housing market. Blacks and Hispanics were shown fewer homes by real estate agents and were more likely to be turned down by loan agencies. Minorities were charged higher prices by agents and lenders and were frequently shown homes only in nonwhite neighborhoods. The result was poorer-quality housing and increased neighborhood segregation for minorities.

In many cities throughout the United States, minorities were intentionally excluded from buying homes in certain neighborhoods.

The practice of refusing to lend money in certain sections of a town or city is called "redlining." Lenders drew red lines around neighborhoods on a map, targeting areas with large minority populations. The lenders then refused to lend in those areas, claiming the borrowers were too high of a risk. Redlining is discriminatory and against the law in the United States, but some lenders have been caught continuing similar practices.

POVERTY MOVES TO THE SUBURBS

Traditionally, large urban centers and small rural communities are most associated with poverty. Since the 1980s, however, poverty has increasingly spread to the suburbs. In the 22-year-period from 1990 to 2012, the poverty rate grew by 43 percent in the suburbs, compared with 17 percent growth in urban centers.[14] In 2015, 16 million individuals lived in poverty in the suburbs— more than in large cities, small metropolitan areas, or rural communities.[15]

The spread of poverty to US suburbs is fueled by several factors. The financial crisis of 2007–2008 resulted in significantly elevated unemployment rates in the suburbs. In addition, since 2000, suburbs have grown at a more rapid pace than cities. Much of the growth is due to poor or low-income inner-city and rural Americans, as well as newly arrived immigrants, flocking to suburbs in search of jobs.

In the past two decades, employment opportunities have shifted away from cities to the suburbs. By 2010, 43 percent of jobs in the country's largest metropolitan areas were located in the suburbs, more than 10 miles (16 km) from a city's center.[16] However, many of the jobs available in the suburbs offer low salaries. Approximately two-thirds of workers in lower-wage jobs, such as food service and preparation, personal care, and janitorial work, live in the suburbs. For these workers, "Moving out provides no guarantee of moving up," said Alan Berube, a deputy director at the Brookings Institution.[17]

Poverty in the United States is not restricted to urban, or even suburban, communities. It strikes rural America as hard, and perhaps even more persistently.

DISCUSSION STARTERS

- Many people who work extremely hard still find themselves in poverty or close to poverty. How important is hard work for avoiding poverty?

- Will poverty in our world always exist? Why or why not?

- More than two million low-income people in the United States live in public housing provided by the federal government. Do you think the US government should provide low-cost housing to these individuals?

FIVE

POVERTY IN
RURAL AMERICA

The Rural Policy Research Institute (RUPRI), an organization that strives to provide information about the needs of rural areas, notes that rural poverty rates have historically been higher compared with urban ones. During the 1950s and 1960s, levels of poverty in rural areas were often twice those in urban areas. According to RUPRI, poverty levels across the entire United States are highest in the most remote rural areas.

The lack of jobs and resulting high levels of unemployment are the leading causes of poverty in rural areas. When the job market declines in urban areas, poor people can sometimes find work in nearby suburbs. In poor rural regions, however, there may be no jobs anywhere.

Mobile homes provide an inexpensive housing option in rural areas.

fertile agricultural land—ranks last of all states by poverty rate. In 2016, nearly 21 percent of all Mississippians lived below the poverty line, as compared with 14 percent nationwide.[4] Residents of the Mississippi delta are among the state's most hard-hit victims of poverty. In some counties, nearly half of the people live in poverty.

Persistent poverty in Mississippi affects the lives of thousands of people every day. Jobs are scarce, and many available jobs are often an hour or more away in factories or processing plants. Ernie, a man in his fifties, says companies won't hire older workers. "There are ways to get by," he says. "Collect cans, do some yard work for a few dollars here and there."[5]

Perhaps the most troubling aspect of economic conditions in the delta is the level of child poverty. Approximately 34 percent of Mississippi children live in poverty, including tens of thousands living in the delta.[6] More than one-half of the 67,000 delta families on food stamps have children.[7]

As they do throughout the world, poverty and poor health go hand in hand in Mississippi. At 9.3 infant deaths per 1,000 live births, in 2015 the state had the highest infant mortality rate in the United States, which has a national average of 5.9 deaths per 1,000 live births. Black infants had nearly twice the mortality rate of white babies.[8]

Some economists view the intense, persistent poverty of the Mississippi delta with pessimism. "If you had to choose between living in a poor village in India and living in the Mississippi Delta . . . I'm not sure who would have the better life," states Angus Deaton, an economist at Princeton University.[9]

THE RIO GRANDE VALLEY

The Rio Grande valley is made up of four counties situated on the southernmost tip of Texas at the border with Mexico. According to the US Census Bureau, approximately one-half of the residents in the valley are living at or below the poverty line.

This old plantation home, just barely standing, is one of many abandoned buildings in the poverty-stricken Mississippi delta.

CHILDREN IN POVERTY[12]

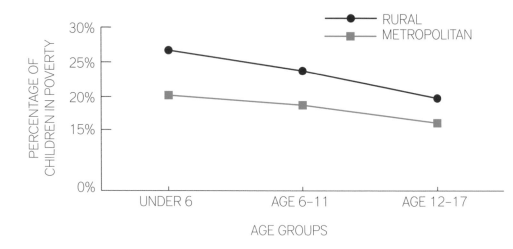

Approximately 90 percent of the valley's population of 1.3 million is Hispanic.[10] Cameron County has the highest child poverty rate in Texas: 47 percent.[11] In 2013, the city of Brownsville in Cameron County was named the poorest city in the United States.

Many people live in colonias, poor communities that often lack basic services such as safe drinking water, electricity, regular garbage pickup, or sewer systems. Typical homes in the approximately 2,300 colonias in Texas are makeshift structures made of materials such as plywood, sheets of tin, and heavy cloth. Many of the residents are undocumented Mexican immigrants who fear the US government will deport them back to Mexico. An undocumented individual is a foreign-born person who does not have the legal right to live or remain in the United States.

Most working people in the colonias hold low-paying jobs in agriculture or manual labor. Approximately 40 percent of the residents need government assistance, such as food stamps, to get by, approximately four times the national average.[13] Undocumented immigrants are not eligible for food stamps and most other federally funded government programs. More than half of the people who live in the colonias do not graduate from high school.

"Sadly, there's a segment of our population [of the Rio Grande valley] that will never be lifted out of poverty," says Pastor Bill Reagan, who runs a shelter and soup kitchen near Brownsville. "They're stuck forever."[14]

RURAL DISABILITY

Rural dwellers make up not only the largest portion of Americans living in poverty but also represent the largest share of Americans who have a disability. Data indicates the disability rate in rural communities is 17.7 percent, compared to 11.8 percent in urban areas. In all, approximately nine million people in rural communities in the United States have disabilities.[15] The higher rate of disability among rural Americans may in part be due to an older population: the percentage of individuals older than 65 is higher in rural areas than in urban areas.

Many rural Americans with disabilities, especially the poor, face a host of challenges. Essential health-care services in rural

A CASE STUDY OF RURAL POVERTY

In the early 1990s, Wanda Turner lived in Blackwell, a county in southwestern Virginia that was once home to a thriving coal mining industry but has been long since plagued by poverty. In 1999, 26-year-old Turner had four children—a 7-month-old baby, a 4-year-old toddler, and 11-year-old twins. Turner's parents were both alcoholics. Her father was a coal miner who left school in the third grade and went to work in the mines as a teenager. When Wanda was 12, her father left his wife and eight children, forcing the family to live on welfare. For years, the family moved from town to town in the coal region.

At 15, Turner got pregnant with the twins and dropped out of high school. Her husband began to drink heavily and was unable to hold a job. The couple moved in with her mother for a brief time, but Turner eventually left her husband. "He wouldn't work, he stayed drunk all the time, and he roughed up the boys. I just got out of it," she said. She moved back to her mother, living with her children in an old trailer. Turner went on Aid to Families with Dependent Children, a former federal program, and also used her mother's food stamps to feed herself and the children. Just as her situation looked bleakest, Turner was accepted into a government assistance program called JOBS. The program bought her new teeth to replace her broken, rotting ones. A caseworker at JOBS encouraged Turner to earn her high school equivalency certificate, but a near lifetime of poverty had tarnished her hopes of improvement. "I don't really look ahead," she said. "I used to did, but I got so disheartened, I just thought, 'Quit dreamin.'"[16]

regions are often scarce. Even when services are available, rural people with disabilities often cannot reach them because of inadequate transportation.

Poverty and unemployment affect the number of people who apply for government disability benefits. Many of these people are jobless, yet still able to work. As a last resort, they apply for disability benefits in the hopes of securing some sort of income. For some, the decision to apply means they have no intention of ever returning to work. "What drives people to [apply for] disability is, in many cases, the repeated loss of work and inability to find new employment," said David Autor, an economist with the Massachusetts Institute of Technology. "Many people who are applying would say, 'Look, I would like to work, but no one would employ me.'"[17]

DISCUSSION STARTERS

- What are some of the common characteristics of rural poverty in the United States? Is rural poverty basically the same everywhere?

- What kind of effect does a healthy farming or mining industry have on rural poverty?

- Do rural people suffer poverty the same way poor people in urban areas do? Explain your answer.

NATIVE AMERICAN
POVERTY

More than one in four American Indians and Alaska Natives live in poverty, according to the Pew Research Center. Native Americans have a higher poverty rate than the national average, but the rate is approximately the same as those of blacks and Hispanics.

The median household income of Native Americans was $39,719 in 2015, compared with $57,564 for the entire nation.[18] Native Americans also have a higher unemployment rate when compared with the national average. In 2015, the Native American unemployment rate was 9.9 percent, the highest in the nation among all races and ethnicities. The jobless rate was double that of whites, 4.6 percent, and significantly higher than the national average of 5.3 percent.[19]

There are approximately 5.2 million Native Americans, making up approximately 2 percent of the total US population. Approximately one-third of the total Native American population lives on one of the 326 federally recognized reservations or government- or Indian-owned tribal lands located on the Great Plains and in the Southwest.

Some experts believe the federal government is to blame for the economic woes Native Americans face, especially on their reservations. Because the government owns reservation lands, Native Americans do not generally own their own homes or land. They are unable to use such assets to get loans to start a business. In addition, the government must approve all development projects on reservations, such as energy development or mining. The process often takes years to complete. "If tribes are given the dignity they deserve," says Shawn Regan, a researcher at the environmental research organization Property and Environment Research Center, "they will have the opportunity to unleash the tremendous wealth of Indian nations."[20]

Native American children experience poverty at higher rates than white children.

SIX

HOMELESSNESS

The US Department of Health and Human Services notes that there are multiple ways a person can be homeless. People can be homeless if they either lack a place of their own in which to sleep at night or sleep in an abandoned building, park, car, or train or bus station. People are also considered homeless if their main place to sleep is a public or private shelter that supplies temporary living space. Also, an individual is homeless if he or she is unable to afford his or her housing and is forced to stay with friends or family.

Homelessness in the United States is not a new phenomenon. It dates to America's earliest colonial settlements in New England and on the East Coast. During the Industrial Revolution of the 1800s, people moved from rural areas to

A homeless man in New York City shares sidewalk space with pigeons.

the cities in search of jobs. Then, as now, there were often not enough jobs for everyone, and many people could not afford housing.

The Civil War (1861–1865) created another surge in America's homeless population. Tens of thousands of veterans were unable to find work upon returning to their cities and villages. Many had suffered physical injuries and trauma during the war, leaving them unable to work. Thousands more become addicted to painkillers taken to recover from wounds or surgeries. Homeless men wandered from town to town or rode the railroads looking for jobs and a permanent residence.

As factories were shuttered in the 1980s, many American workers lost decent-paying jobs. The service industry jobs that were available often didn't pay enough to cover housing costs.

In the 1980s, homelessness reached epidemic proportions. The service industry—a traditionally lower-paying sector—replaced manufacturing as the number one source of jobs. More than 75 percent of the new jobs created during the 1980s were minimum wage positions.[1] Funds for government public housing programs were slashed, and the supply of affordable housing plummeted nationwide. In a survey of 182 US cities with populations more than 100,000, homeless rates tripled from 1981 to 1989.[2]

Today the United States faces a daunting challenge. Homelessness is growing around the country, devastating its victims and affecting the wider society. Who are America's homeless, and how bad is the problem?

HOOVERVILLES

During the Great Depression, an economic downturn that began in 1929 and lasted approximately ten years, millions lost their jobs. Homeowners lost their properties because they were unable to pay their mortgages or pay taxes. Renters could not keep up payments and were forced out of their apartments. As the Great Depression worsened, many of these people began living in the streets, setting up shantytowns in cities across the United States. The impoverished, unsanitary settlements were called Hoovervilles, after then president Herbert Hoover. The shanties were thrown together with cardboard, sheets of tin, glass, and any other materials people could find. A single Hooverville in a large metropolitan area, such as New York City, was home to thousands of people. President Franklin D. Roosevelt, elected in 1932, launched the economic recovery program called the New Deal, which helped reduce unemployment. By the early 1940s, many of the Hoovervilles had been removed.

THE HOMELESS IN AMERICA

Homelessness cuts across all segments of American society, affecting single adults, children and families, veterans, youth and young adults, and the chronically homeless. No race, ethnicity, or religion is immune to the effects of homelessness.

According to the National Alliance to End Homelessness, on any given night in 2015, approximately 565,000 people were homeless, either sleeping outside or in a shelter or temporary housing program. The national rate of homelessness per 10,000 people in 2015 was 17.7 people, ranging from 111 in Washington, DC, to 7 in Mississippi.[3] The low rate of homelessness in Mississippi is due to its overall low housing costs.

Homeless people are found in every region of the country, in every type of community. Approximately 49 percent of

Many people resort to living in their cars when they don't have enough money to pay for permanent housing.

people experiencing homelessness in the United States in 2016 lived in major cities. Smaller cities were home to approximately 37 percent of the homeless, while rural counties accounted for approximately 14 percent of the total homeless population.[4]

SINGLE ADULTS

Most people who experience homelessness are single adults. In 2017, nearly 370,000 single adults were homeless on any given night. In 2016, on any given night in California, more than 118,000 people experienced homelessness. In New York State, that number was 86,000, while in Florida it was 34,000. In Texas, 23,000 people were homeless on any given night, and Washington State had 21,000 people who were homeless. New York City, with 60,000 homeless, and Los Angeles, California, with 57,000 homeless, have the second- and third-most homeless people of all cities in the world.[5] The capital of the Philippines, Manila, has more people that are homeless than in any other city in the world.

FAMILY HOUSEHOLDS

On any given night in 2017, nearly 185,000 people in families—or 58,000 family households—were homeless. Sixty-two percent, or 121,000, were children younger than six years old.[6] Large numbers of these homeless families lived on the street or in other places not intended to be living spaces. Like other groups who experience homelessness, homeless families usually are

The US Department of Veterans Affairs tries to find homes for veterans, but it cannot help all of them.

jobless and earn incomes less than they need to pay for housing. Single mothers with low education and young children are the heads of many homeless families.

VETERANS

US soldiers returning from combat in Iraq and Afghanistan have pushed the number of homeless veterans to near-record highs. Those who served in the Vietnam War (1955–1975) also make up a significant proportion of homeless vets. Many veterans have suffered physical injury, including brain trauma and the loss of limbs. Others are victims of post-traumatic stress disorder (PTSD), a condition brought on by having experienced a terrifying or damaging event.

Ronald Frankford, a homeless veteran living in New Orleans, Louisiana, was wounded in Vietnam in 1969. He was awarded several medals for his service, including the Purple Heart, which is awarded to soldiers who have been wounded or killed in combat. Frankford suffered from PTSD and had been homeless for 12 years when he was interviewed in 2010. He said, "The Veterans Administration is trying to help me, but every time I feel like I'm getting help, I just leave. I get paranoid, schizophrenic."[7]

Frankford's condition made it difficult for him to hold a

HOMELESS WOMEN VETERANS

Women make up approximately 10 percent of the total US veteran population and approximately 9 percent of all US veterans who are homeless. Like their male counterparts, many of the returning women vets suffer from mental health problems and drug or alcohol abuse. Some were the victims of violent sexual crimes while serving in the armed forces. These veterans may find it difficult to hold a job, thus increasing the threat of homelessness. Approximately three-quarters of homeless female veterans are unemployed, largely due to a lack of accessible and affordable childcare. In many cases, the temporary housing available to homeless women veterans through government programs is unsafe. Several facilities do not properly segregate male and female residents, resulting in safety and security concerns for the women veterans.

LGBT HOMELESS YOUTH

A significant portion of the homeless youth served by shelters are LGBT individuals. LGBT youth are at high risk of homelessness for a variety of reasons, including family rejection, abuse, or financial or emotional neglect. In shelters, LGBT youth are often harassed or suffer abuse by other residents or shelter staff. As a result, LGBT youth are more likely to live on the streets than heterosexual youth. The National Coalition for the Homeless reports transgender people are often turned away from shelters. In some instances, signs are posted barring their admittance.

steady job and find a permanent residence. "I'm scared to death of reality. I don't know how to cope with it. Sometimes I'd rather try to commit suicide than stay alive, to tell the truth."[8]

YOUTH AND YOUNG ADULTS

Family turmoil, poverty, pregnancy, and parental substance abuse are major contributing factors to youth and young adult homelessness. Between 20 percent and 40 percent of homeless youth identify themselves as lesbian, gay, bisexual, or transgender (LGBT).[9] Many young individuals who are homeless lived in multiple home settings: some were in foster care, whereas others lived with friends or nonparent family members.

On any given night in 2017, there were nearly 41,000 homeless youths and young adults on the streets in the United States. Twelve percent were younger than 18; the remaining 88 percent were age 18 to 24.[10] Black and Native American youth are more likely to become homeless than their white and

CHOOSING TO LIVE ON THE STREETS

Thousands of homeless people in the United States live in homeless shelters run by cities, churches, or private welfare groups. Living conditions vary from shelter to shelter, from decent rooms that house a few residents to larger spaces filled with dozens of bunk beds and warehouse-sized areas with only blankets and sleeping bags sprawled across the floor. Many homeless shelters are unsafe and poorly managed. Feeling endangered, many homeless people choose to live on the streets. They may sleep in parks, under bridges, in railroad and bus terminals, in abandoned buildings, and even underground in subway tunnels.

David Pirtle, a man made homeless in 2004 due to a psychological disorder, said, "Shelters are dangerous places . . . they're full of drugs and drug dealers . . . people will steal your shoes, and there's bedbugs and body lice. . . . A lot of those things are true." Because of these dangers, Pirtle chose to live on the streets, even on the coldest nights when he risked freezing to death. "My fear of the unknown, of what might be waiting for me at that shelter, was worse than my fear of the known risk, you know, of staying out on the street. . . . We get comfortable in the most uncomfortable positions, and that just becomes home."[11] In time, Pirtle got treatment for his disorder and slowly recovered. No longer homeless, he began working for the National Coalition for the Homeless and became an advocate for the rights of homeless people and those with mental illness.

Hispanic counterparts. Young homeless people often engage in high-risk behaviors, such as exchanging sex for food, clothing, and shelter. Many youth and young adults experience high rates of anxiety, depression, suicide, and poor health.

THE CAUSES OF HOMELESSNESS

Unemployment, poverty, and the widespread lack of affordable housing are the leading causes of homelessness. Domestic violence, drug and alcohol abuse, and mental or physical disabilities also add to the likelihood of homelessness.

A TIMELINE OF GOVERNMENT AID FOR THE HOMELESS

Efforts by the federal government to aid the homeless began in earnest in 1892 when Congress authorized the Labor Department to study slum conditions in the four major US cities with populations higher than 200,000 people. In 1908, a presidentially appointed Housing Commission suggested the government buy slum properties to rebuild or renovate them. Other government programs to help the homeless followed:

- 1932: In the throes of the Great Depression, the government-established Reconstruction Finance Corporation lent money to private companies to build housing for low-income families.

- 1933: The Public Works Administration used federal funds to clear slums and build low-cost housing; approximately 40,000 new units were built.

- 1937: The US Housing Act of 1937 established special agencies to develop low-rent housing programs throughout the country.

- 1946: The Farmers Home Administration was created to provide low-income housing aid in rural areas.

- 1949: The Housing Act of 1949 authorized and funded the clearing of slums to build 810,000 public housing units.

- 1968: The Housing and Urban Development Act (HUD) was adopted to build 26 million new units for low- and moderate-income families.

- 1987: The McKinney Homelessness Assistance Act granted HUD funding to provide emergency shelters to homeless Americans.

- 2009: The American Recovery and Reinvestment Act earmarked $1.5 billion for homelessness prevention and rent assistance.

For women, domestic violence is the leading cause of homelessness. More than 80 percent of homeless women with children are the victims of domestic violence. Homeless mothers experience a range of physical and emotional disorders. They experience three times the national rate of PTSD and twice the rate of drug and alcohol addiction. Approximately one-half of mothers reported depression since becoming homeless, and they experience ulcers at four times the rate of other women.

The National Coalition for the Homeless reports that approximately 16 percent of the single-adult homeless population has a severe and persistent mental illness. Approximately 26 percent of adults living in shelters have serious psychiatric disorders.[12] Because homeless individuals with mental illness often do not have access to proper treatment, it is difficult for them to get back to normal housing. Therefore, they begin to experience chronic homelessness, living on the streets or in shelters year after year.

Homelessness is one of the most extreme consequences of poverty. Poverty also has far-reaching effects on a person's health and health care.

DISCUSSION STARTERS

- Do you think hard work is the most effective way of escaping homelessness? Why or why not?

- What would you do if you saw a homeless person on the street? What type of assistance, if any, would you offer him or her?

- Imagine being homeless. How would you handle the fear of being hungry, cold, or alone? What would you do to keep going or improve your conditions?

SEVEN

HEALTH, HEALTH CARE, AND POVERTY

Being poor affects the quality of an individual's physical and emotional health. Being poor increases your risk of becoming sick, becoming disabled, or dying prematurely. The poor are also less likely to have access to quality medical care and less likely to have knowledge about health issues and related information such as nutrition. The poor are likely to be obese and more likely to be addicted to tobacco, drugs, and alcohol. Ultimately, poor health increases the risk that a poor person will remain poor.

HOW BAD IS BAD?

The effects of poverty can have long-term effects on a person's health. Poverty affects both the young and old, but it can be

The stresses of living in poverty, such as not having enough to eat and living in unhealthy conditions, can cause physical and mental illnesses.

particularly harmful in infants and children. The poor face higher rates of heart disease, diabetes, cancer, infant mortality, high blood pressure, and asthma. The death rate for the poor between age 25 and 64 is nearly three times higher than for the wealthy among the same age range.[1] The poor have a lower life expectancy, too. The richest one percent of Americans lives an average of nearly 15 years longer than the poorest one percent.[2]

The emotional stresses of living in poverty—joblessness, homelessness, the threat of violence, and unhealthy physical environments—often result in debilitating mental disorders. According to the National Survey of Drug Use and Health, approximately 2.5 million adults in the United States living below the poverty line had a serious mental illness in 2016.[3] Adults age 26 or older living below the poverty line were more than twice as likely to experience a serious mental illness than those living above the poverty line.

THE FOOD GAP

According to a study by the Harvard School of Public Health in 2014, the diet quality of high-income families is improving, but it is declining among low-income families. The so-called "food gap" in America is widening at an alarming rate. Frank Hu, a professor of nutrition at Harvard and one of the study's researchers, said the growing gap between the haves and have-nots is "disturbing." Evidence indicates that there is a definite link between poverty and obesity. "The answer is pretty simple," said Dr. Benard Dreyer, president of the American Academy of Pediatrics. "The cheapest food you can buy is usually empty calories— high-calorie, high-fat food."[4]

Data gathered from a low-income housing development in Chicago indicated that poor youth experienced short-term anxiety at nearly three times the rate of the general US population and long-term anxiety and nervousness at nearly seven times the rate of the general US population. Adults from the same housing development experienced elevated worry nearly five times the national average and depression more than three times the national average.

Escaping stress is as challenging a task as escaping poverty itself. "They [the poor] live in more dangerous environments," says Dr. Benard Dreyer, president of the American Academy of Pediatrics. "They live in substandard housing. They live in dangerous neighborhoods where they can be shot or injured."[5]

Soup kitchens work to fill the nutritional gap for homeless and impoverished families.

CHILDREN AT RISK

Approximately one-half of all children in the United States live in poverty or near poverty. Even before they are born, children who experience poverty are at greater risk for a broad range of problems related to physical health, emotional development, and educational achievement. Poverty increases the risk for low birth weight, infant mortality, and chronic childhood illness. Poor children are also more likely to suffer from severe asthma, as well as diarrhea or colitis. They have significantly higher rates of iron deficiency and are more likely to suffer from blindness or deafness.

A contributing cause to these ailments is a lack of adequate nutrition. The US Department of Agriculture estimates that more than 14 million children are food insecure.[6] Food insecurity is not having consistent access to enough healthful food. Without proper nutrition, children are at risk for more frequent coughs, colds, ear infections, and fevers. Malnutrition can also lead to

OLDER ADULTS AND HEALTH CARE

More than 25 million people age 60 and older live on the borderline of poverty.[7] These senior Americans struggle to pay rent and health-care bills, such as any costs not covered by Medicare. The average older adult pays more than $4,700 annually in out-of-pocket health-care costs.[8] Yet the sole income of many seniors is their Social Security benefit, approximately $1,350 per month for an individual retired worker.[9] The high cost of health care puts many older adults at greater risk of homelessness. In 2014, more than 300,000 people over age 50 were homeless.[10]

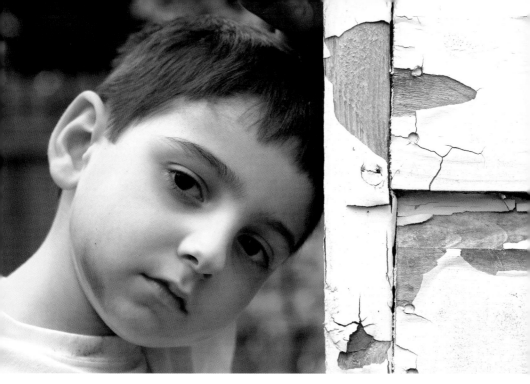

Consistent exposure to peeling lead paint can cause serious health problems for children.

poor brain development and behavioral problems such as aggression, anxiety, and depression.

Each year in the United States, more than 300,000 children age one to five have unsafe levels of lead, a poisonous metal, in their blood.[11] Being poor increases the risk of lead poisoning because of the often toxic, hazardous environments in which poor children live. Though lead-based paint was banned in 1978, it still remains in millions of homes in the United States. Unaware of the dangers, infants and young children often ingest flaking and peeling lead-based paint, either eating the flakes or breathing in the dust in the air that is filled with lead paint particles.

High levels of lead in the blood can have devastating effects on children. Lead poisoning can lead to decreased bone and muscle growth, damage to organs, hearing and vision problems, and seizures, among other ailments. Lower IQ scores, attention disorders, and speech, language, and reading problems have also been linked to high lead levels.

"There's no safe level of lead exposure," says Dr. James Duffee of Springfield, Ohio, who serves mostly low-income children and families. "Exposure to lead in the first couple of years can cause lifelong, irreparable damage to the brain."[12]

POVERTY AND HEALTH CARE

The relationship between poverty and adequate health care is a frustrating cycle that keeps those most in need of care from

A young boy waits to get a flu shot at a free clinic. These pop-up clinics are one way families without health insurance receive preventative care.

obtaining it. Poverty is both a major cause of bad health and an obstacle to accessing health care. The poor often cannot afford to buy those things that contribute to good health, such as proper nutrition and clean, safe housing. In turn, bad health can cause poverty. If an individual suffers long-term physical or psychological illness, he or she may be unable to hold down steady employment. In such a case, poverty may be just around the corner.

Lack of health care is a major challenge to people living in poverty. Unable to afford proper care, the poor often leave their health problems untreated. Nearly 70 percent of people without health insurance in the United States are poor or near poor. In 2014, 7 percent of children living below the poverty line were uninsured, whereas 25 percent of adults living below the poverty line were uninsured.[13]

For most Americans, health insurance is the best means to access health care. Many

MEDICAID AND MEDICARE

Medicaid is a federal- and state-run medical assistance program for low-income individuals and families of all ages. Some of the health-care services covered under Medicaid include doctors, hospitals, home health-care, X-rays, laboratory tests, and rural health clinics, among others. People who qualify for the program usually pay none of the costs of their medical expenses. Some service providers, however, require a small co-payment. Medicare is a federal health insurance program for individuals 65 or older and for people who have certain disabilities. Medicare covers many of the same services covered by Medicaid.

NEGATIVE STEREOTYPES

Many patients insured by government medical assistance programs, such as Medicaid, report negative experiences when they use health-care services. In a study reported in 2014 in *Milbank Quarterly*, a journal focusing on health issues, patients described their humiliating experiences at doctor's offices, hospitals, and clinics.

"I think that the kind of insurance you have identifies you as what kind of group you fall in," said one patient. "[Having Medicaid puts me into the] broke, poor class, the class that is welfare class. The doctor who's sitting there, he's definitely upper class. Probably see me coming in and says, 'Man, I'm paying for this.'"

Others believed they were treated disrespectfully because they were poor. A woman visited a doctor to get an important test. She explained, "I felt like I was being judged for not having health insurance. . . . I didn't like how he made me feel at all. . . . I was supposed to reschedule an appointment. But since he was rude to me, I didn't reschedule that appointment."

Negative stereotypes of the poor are likely to affect the patient's long-term physical health. One patient said, "What happens with people that live on an income such as I do is that when other people start talking down to you, you don't want to hear any more because you don't want to feel bad about yourself so you shut down or don't ask questions."[14]

businesses offer their employees health insurance benefits. In recent years, businesses have cut back this practice to reduce their costs. Individuals or families not covered by a workplace buy private health insurance plans from insurance companies. The plans allow the buyer to visit hospitals, doctors, and dentists at reduced fees. The plans also provide coverage for prescription drugs.

Poor families, however, may be unable to afford private health insurance. The unemployed poor, of course, do not have employers to provide them with insurance. Some may have access to Medicaid or Medicare, government-run health insurance programs, but not all poor people qualify. Those who do not are uninsured. The costs of their health care must come out of their own pockets.

Struggling to pay rent and buy food, clothing, and other basics with limited funds, the poor often cannot take care of their own health or the health of their children. In fact, studies have shown that compared with children living at twice the poverty level, poor children are more likely to have not seen a doctor in at least five years and more likely to have a medical need untreated. "Insurance is not just supposed to get you access to care, it's supposed to keep you from getting evicted from your apartment because you paid your hospital bill instead of your rent," explains Katherine Baicker, professor of health economics at the Harvard Chan School of Public Health.[15]

DISCUSSION STARTERS

- Research the term *food desert* on the internet. How do food deserts affect poor people in the United States?

- The US government operates the National School Lunch Program to provide nutritional meals to schoolchildren. Do you think taxpayer dollars should be used to feed children, or should it be the responsibility of the children's families? Explain.

- Think about the emotional stresses of living in poverty. What strategies might you use to cope with this stress? How could you help someone else coping with this stress?

EIGHT

EDUCATION AND
POVERTY

C hildren living in poverty are more likely to perform at a lower academic level than children who are not poor. They are more likely to receive lower grades and test scores, more likely to drop out of high school, and less likely to attend college. Children living in poverty have a higher rate of absenteeism than nonpoor children, and they are more likely to quit school to work or care for a family member. Poor children are more likely to experience developmental problems or learning disabilities than those who don't live in poverty. Less than one-half of poor children are ready for school at age five, compared with 75 percent of those from nonpoor households.[1]

Children living in poverty are less likely than their peers to be ready for kindergarten.

THE EDUCATION GAP

Most of the public school districts across the United States are run by local communities and are financed by local property taxes. In wealthy communities, property tax revenues are higher because the property is worth more, meaning these areas can generate more money for schools and education. The homes in high-poverty areas have lower value and therefore generate less taxes. Well-financed schools in wealthier districts can afford new textbooks, up-to-date equipment, computers, and teaching specialists such as guidance counselors and speech therapists. Schools in poor districts often have outdated equipment, larger class sizes, and fewer specialists, resulting in a poorer education for the poorer students. The wealthy town of Greenwich, Connecticut, for example, spends $6,000 more per pupil than the high-poverty village of Bridgeport, Connecticut—a community less than 30 miles (48 km) away.[3]

ARE THE SCHOOLS A PROBLEM?

The chronic stresses of poverty affect a child's intellectual and emotional development, often leading to substandard educational performance. But are schools themselves part of the reason children living in poverty are likely to do poorly? According to experts, in many cases, they are—especially when it concerns minority groups.

In 2014, 43 percent of black and Hispanic students attending US public schools were in high-poverty schools, while approximately 8 percent of white students were.[2] A high-poverty school is one where at least three-quarters of students are poor or low income. High-poverty schools are often underfunded and inadequately staffed. This results in an inferior educational experience for students already struggling with poverty.

Ultimately, the poverty of the schools themselves frequently denies the students a quality education. "They are in poor communities, they have less local resources, they have fewer parents with college degrees, they have fewer two-parent families where there are parents who can come spend time volunteering in the school, they have a harder time attracting the best teachers," says Sean Reardon, a professor of education at Stanford University. "So for a lot of reasons schools serving poor kids tend to have fewer economic and social capital resources."[4]

In response to the concentration of poverty in US public schools, several cities have implemented plans to level the playing field for all students. In Dallas, Texas, more than 83 percent of black students and 88 percent of Hispanic students are enrolled in high-poverty schools.[5] Working to prepare younger students for college and high-skilled jobs, Dallas launched a groundbreaking program that offers a bonus to its best teachers to teach at struggling, high-poverty schools.

"Some claim the education problem can't be overcome without first breaking the cycle of poverty," says Todd Williams, director of Commit! Partnership, an organization that seeks to improve education in Dallas. "That's akin to dismissing the power of effective educators while throwing up our hands and saying 'we can't be better.'"[6]

GETTING A HEAD START

Head Start is a federal government program that helps prepare children from low-income families for school. The program focuses on children from birth to age five. Launched in 1965, Head Start promotes language and literacy development as well as providing health and nutritional services to the children. The program began as a half-day, eight-week test project but has since grown to become a full-day, year-round service. Head Start gets parents involved, encouraging them to play an active role in their children's development. The Head Start curriculum varies from community to community, but the primary focus in most cases is getting kids ready to start school.

A typical Head Start day begins at approximately eight o'clock in a school classroom. Classes usually have fewer than 20 children. Learning begins immediately, as the children prepare for breakfast. They wash their hands, serve food from containers, and use forks and spoons—tasks that help build language and motor skills. The environment is playful and lively, with teachers, parent volunteers, and children interacting closely with one another. In-class lessons include recognizing shapes and colors and learning the alphabet and numbers. During recess, children are able to play on the playground, where they not only get exercise but also learn communication and social skills. Since its beginning, Head Start has served more than 32 million children.[11]

The teachers polled recommended that school districts hire a full-time trained administrator who would work inside schools and help low-income students and their family members solve nonacademic problems.

SUCCESSFUL HIGH-POVERTY SCHOOLS

Though the state of high-poverty schools is discouraging, not all schools in poor communities are low performing. Despite tight budgets and inadequate environments, many high-poverty schools in the United States beat the odds and achieve remarkable success. In these schools, low-income students match or exceed the scores attained by their counterparts in higher-income schools on standardized tests.

Studies show that high-performing, high-poverty schools differ from lower-performing schools in several key areas. In high-performing schools, teachers believe that all students can succeed at high levels. School administrators and teachers maintain a strong work ethic, and teachers accept their roles in the success or failure of the students. Racial and gender diversity and equality are also prominent features of successful high-poverty schools. An encouraging conclusion to draw from high-performing, high-poverty schools is that schools in areas of greatest hardship can be places where children can learn and excel academically.

DISCUSSION STARTERS

- What would you do to encourage fewer school absences among low-income students?

- How can high-poverty schools work with students' families and the community to attain higher performance?

- How would you help teachers in high-poverty schools learn how to better connect with students living in poverty?

NINE

FIGHTING
POVERTY TODAY

T oday, the federal government confronts poverty in the United States with many initiatives that are collectively referred to as the safety net. The safety net consists of 13 programs that provide cash, grants, food, child care, job training, and housing for qualifying low-income individuals and families. It also includes Medicaid. The programs are funded by taxpayers and overseen by various federal government agencies.

After Medicaid, tax credits account for the largest spending of all the safety net welfare programs. These credits reduce the amount of taxes owed by low-income workers. They include the Earned Income Tax Credit (EITC) and the Child Tax Credit (CTC).

Many people have participated in rallies to show their support for Social Security and Medicare.

To qualify for the EITC, families must have earned income from a job and must not have earned more than a specified amount of money. The CTC provides an additional credit per each child younger than 17.

The Supplemental Nutrition Assistance Program (SNAP), formerly known as the Food Stamp Program, provides participants with a monthly debit card that can be used to buy food in most grocery stores. The cards cannot be used to purchase nonfood items.

There are other programs in the federal safety net. One program is Temporary Assistance for Needy Families (TANF), which is a joint federal and state program that provides cash to assist needy families with childcare, pregnancy prevention, and educational activities. Another program is Supplemental Security Income (SSI). In this program, cash is

REPRESENTING THE POOR

Since the 1800s, independent legal aid organizations have been providing legal assistance for poor people in the United States. The poor often have had limited access to lawyers and little knowledge of the legal system. In 1965, the OEO created the Legal Services Program, part of the Johnson administration's War on Poverty. Today the program is known as the Legal Services Corporation. The program offers free services to low-income people, representing them in court cases involving health, housing, and employment problems, among other matters. Legal Services lawyers have won important decisions that ensure welfare recipients are not denied benefits. They also fight to protect the rights of consumers and poor tenants.

paid to those who are blind, disabled, or older than 65. Lifeline, another safety net program, provides up to $9.25 a month to help low-income people pay home or cell phone costs.

CUTS TO COME?

Soon after taking office in January 2017, President Donald Trump proposed severe cuts to anti-poverty and health-care programs used by millions of low-income Americans. Those programs include TANF, SNAP, and the Children's Health Insurance Program, or CHIP. CHIP provides low-cost health coverage to children up to age 19 in families that earn too much money to qualify for Medicaid but not enough to purchase private health insurance. In his budget, President Trump proposed slashing approximately $193 billion from SNAP alone in the course of ten years.[1]

During his first year in office, President Trump worked to overturn President Barack Obama's health-care plan and made cuts to programs designed to help the poor, in an effort to reduce federal spending.

In January 2018, the Trump administration issued guidelines to states that allowed them to deny Medicaid benefits to people who do not have jobs. People who attend school or are involved in certain types of community activities would be exempt from the new policy. Since Medicaid was founded, the program has never had work requirements. The administration's objectives are to prevent healthy, able-bodied people from taking advantage of the Medicaid system and to provide people with an incentive to work. Critics of the plan point to research that shows that at least 6.3 million Americans would risk losing their health care under these changes. Approximately 60 percent of adults who receive Medicaid benefits already have jobs. Of those who are not working, more than one-third are disabled or ill.[2]

Whether the proposed cuts will be implemented remained to be seen in early 2018. The administration's attempts to reduce federal spending by slashing benefits to low-income Americans will be challenged

AMERICA'S HEALTHIER CHILDREN

In 2010, Congress passed the Healthy, Hunger-Free Kids Act to ensure that children had access to nutritious, balanced breakfasts and lunches during the school day. The goal of the program, spearheaded by then First Lady Michelle Obama, was to help reduce child obesity and decrease health risks for America's children. The act authorized the US Department of Agriculture to make changes to school food programs that would add healthier food choices to the school menu. Studies to determine the effectiveness of the program show that children are eating more fruits and vegetables, while enjoying a diet that contains less sugar, fat, and sodium.

Food-shelf volunteers help sort and pack food for those in need.

by members of the Democratic Party in Congress. Actions that states take to impose work requirements on Medicaid are sure to be tested in the courts.

PEOPLE HELPING PEOPLE

Thousands of nongovernmental groups throughout the United States have joined the fight to reduce poverty and serve the needy. Food banks and anti-hunger organizations gather food from local residents and businesses and distribute it to individuals and families in need. Organizations such as the Children's Hunger Alliance in Ohio, the Rhode Island Community Food Bank, and Feeding America are just a handful of the many groups that provide healthy meals and snacks for low-income children and adults. Church, synagogue, and mosque outreach programs, soup kitchens, and shelters for the homeless also help alleviate the hardships of poverty.

Poverty can be reduced. Creating more jobs, sustaining the social safety net, and investing in high-quality education have proven to be effective ways to combat poverty. Nor is the outlook completely bleak.

EVERYONE CAN MAKE A DIFFERENCE

Tens of thousands of American citizens have dedicated their efforts to fighting poverty in different, personal ways. Here are a few ways people help:

- Writing their representatives and senators to stop cuts to anti-poverty programs.
- Donating food, clothing, books, and toys to local shelters and programs.
- Volunteering to work at a shelter, serving food, spending time with families, or reading to children.
- Making a fundraising plan or hosting activities to raise donations for worthy anti-poverty organizations.

WORDS OF HOPE

Muhammad Yunus, born in Bangladesh, is an economist and social activist. He was awarded the 2006 Nobel Peace Prize for his efforts to create economic development for those in need. He also received the Presidential Medal of Freedom in 2009 and the Congressional Gold Medal in 2010, the two highest civilian honors in the United States. Yunus has written several books on poverty and its effects on world society. In *Creating a World Without Poverty*, he writes, "Once poverty is gone, we'll need to build museums to display its horrors to future generations. They'll wonder why poverty continued so long in human society—how a few people could live in luxury while billions dwelt in misery, deprivation and despair."[4]

An encouraging sign is that poverty in the United States fell from 14.8 percent in 2014 to 12.7 percent in 2016, a decrease of more than 6.7 million people.[3]

Yet this still means that as the twenty-first century unfolds, more than 41 million Americans continue to suffer in poverty. There is much work that remains to be done.

DISCUSSION STARTERS

- Do you think the United States has done enough to combat poverty? Explain your answer.

- In your opinion, have welfare programs helped to reduce poverty in America? Why or why not?

- What reforms would you make to safety net welfare programs to make them more effective?

ESSENTIAL FACTS

SIGNIFICANT EVENTS

- In 1962, Michael Harrington published the book *The Other America: Poverty in the United States*, which called attention to the widespread poverty in the United States.

- In January 1964, President Johnson called for an "unconditional war on poverty" in his State of the Union address. A series of laws were enacted to end poverty and improve living conditions for Americans. Congress passed the Economic Opportunity Act in 1964. In April 1965, the Elementary and Secondary Education Act was adopted, and in May, Head Start was launched. In 1968, the Housing and Urban Development Act (HUD) authorized 26 million new units for low- and moderate-income families to be built.

- In 2009, Congress passed the American Recovery and Reinvestment Act, which earmarked $1.5 billion for homelessness prevention and rent assistance for the poor.

- The Healthy, Hunger-Free Kids Act was passed in 2010 to ensure schoolchildren had access to nutritious breakfasts and lunches.

KEY PLAYERS

- Lyndon B. Johnson, the thirty-sixth president of the United States, launched the federal government's War on Poverty, the cornerstone of his vision for a Great Society.

- Michael Harrington was the author of *The Other America: Poverty in the United States*, an influential book that revealed the depths of poverty, from rural Appalachia to US inner cities.

- Rev. Dr. Martin Luther King Jr., an African American minister and civil rights activist, pressured the government to focus on the War on Poverty instead of the war in Vietnam.

IMPACT ON SOCIETY

The effects of poverty on individuals, families, and American society are devastating. Poverty is closely linked to poor academic achievement, high crime rates, and a host of health-related issues. Poverty affects children most severely, resulting in poor cognitive development and an increased likelihood of suffering from mental illness in later years compared with people who did not grow up in poverty. Poor nutrition, lack of medical care, homelessness, and an unstable family life are additional by-products of poverty in America.

QUOTE

"Tens of millions of Americans are, at this very moment, maimed in body and spirit, existing at levels beneath those necessary for human decency. If these people are not starving, they are hungry, and sometimes fat with hunger, for that is what cheap foods do. They are without adequate housing and education and medical care."

—*Michael Harrington,* The Other America: Poverty in the United States, *1962*

GLOSSARY

ACTIVIST
A person who campaigns to bring about political or social change.

BANKRUPTCY
The state of being unable to pay debts.

CHRONIC
Continuing for a long time.

COGNITIVE
Related to the act or process of thinking, reasoning, remembering, imagining, or learning.

COST OF LIVING
The amount of money needed to live at a particular standard of well-being.

FOOD INSECURITY
The state of not having consistent access to enough food for an active, healthy life.

HOUSEHOLD
A group of people, related or unrelated, who live at the same address.

INFANT MORTALITY RATE
The percentage of children younger than one year who die divided by the number of live births that year.

INFLATION
An increase in the price of goods and services.

MEDIAN HOUSEHOLD INCOME
The income level in the middle of ranked incomes.

MORTGAGE
A legal agreement by which a bank or other creditor lends money at interest in exchange for taking title of the debtor's property.

PUBLIC HOUSING
Housing the government owns, operates, or sponsors that has low rent.

REVENUE
Income, especially of a company or organization and of a substantial nature.

SERVICE INDUSTRY
A class of businesses that do work for a customer, and occasionally provide goods, but are not involved in manufacturing.

SHANTYTOWN
A collection of huts in which poor people live, usually in or near a large city.

UNCONDITIONAL
Absolute; without limitations.

WELFARE
Financial support provided by the government to people in need.

ADDITIONAL
RESOURCES

SELECTED BIBLIOGRAPHY

Allen, Wilmot. "Urban Poverty in America: The Truly Disadvantaged Revisited." *Huffington Post*. Huffington Post, 25 Aug. 2014. Web. 6 Dec. 2017.

Iceland, John. *Poverty in America: A Handbook*. Berkeley, CA: U of California P, 2013. Print.

Rank, Mark Robert. *One Nation, Underprivileged: Why American Poverty Affects Us All*. New York: Oxford UP, 2005. Print.

Rodd, Scott. "This Is What Poverty Looks Like." *ThinkProgress*. ThinkProgress, 11 Mar. 2015. Web. 7 Dec. 2017.

FURTHER READINGS

Laine, Carolee. *The War on Poverty*. Minneapolis: Abdo, 2017. Print.

Riis, Jacob. *How the Other Half Lives*. Eastford, CT: Martino Fine, 2015. Print.

ONLINE RESOURCES

Booklinks
NONFICTION NETWORK
FREE! ONLINE NONFICTION RESOURCES

To learn more about being poor in America, visit **abdobooklinks.com**. These links are routinely monitored and updated to provide the most current information available.

MORE INFORMATION

For more information on this subject, contact or visit the following organizations:

HEARTLAND ALLIANCE
208 S. LaSalle Street, Suite 1300
Chicago, IL 60604
312-660-1300
heartlandalliance.org

Heartland Alliance works to help people who are homeless, living in poverty, or seeking safety by providing health, housing, jobs, and justice.

NATIONAL LOW INCOME HOUSING COALITION (NLIHC)
1000 Vermont Avenue, Suite 500
Washington, DC 20005
202-662-1530
nlihc.org

The NLIHC is dedicated to developing government policies that ensure people with the lowest incomes in the United States have affordable and decent housing.

NATIONAL STUDENT CAMPAIGN AGAINST HUNGER AND HOMELESSNESS
294 Washington Street, Suite 500
Boston, MA 02108
studentsagainsthunger.org

The NSCAHH is committed to ending hunger and homelessness by educating and training students to meet people's needs while advocating for long-term solutions.

POVERTY & RACE RESEARCH ACTION COUNCIL (PRRAC)
740 Fifteenth Street NW, Suite 300
Washington, DC 20005
prrac.org/about.php

The PRRAC is a civil rights policy organization that works to improve housing and education opportunities for low-income families.

SOURCE NOTES

CHAPTER 1. THE AMERICAN WAY OF POVERTY

1. *Student Dictionary*. Boston: Houghton Mifflin, 1998. Print. 750.

2. Joseph Connors and James D. Gwartney. "Changes in Poverty Rates by the Numbers." *Common Sense Economics*. Common Sense Economics, n.d. Web. 6 Mar. 2018.

3. Karen Seccombe. *Families in Poverty*. New York: Ally and Bacon, 2007. Print. 33.

4. "Poverty Thresholds." *Census Bureau*. USCB, n.d. Web. 26 Nov. 2017.

5. "Income and Poverty in the United States: 2016." *Census Bureau*. USCB, n.d. Web. 27 Nov. 2017.

6. "Income and Poverty in the United States: 2016."

7. "Facts for Features: American Indian and Alaska Native Heritage Month: November 2015." *Census Bureau*. USCB, n.d. Web. 22 Jan. 2018.

8. Annie Lowrey. "America's Child Poverty Rate." *Atlantic*. Atlantic, 5 Oct. 2017. Web. 6 Dec. 2017.

9. Marian Wright Edelman. "The High Moral and Economic Cost of Child Poverty in America." *Children's Defense Fund*. Children's Defense Fund, 19 Sept. 2014. Web. 6 Dec. 2017.

10. "The War on Poverty Has Cost $22 Trillion." *National Center for Policy Analysis*. NCPA, Web. 27 Nov. 2017.

CHAPTER 2. THE CAUSES AND FACTORS OF POVERTY

1. "What Is Poverty?" *Economic and Social Inclusion Corporation*. Government of New Brunswick, Canada, n.d. Web. 5 Dec. 2017.

2. Jie Zong, Jeanne Batalova, and Jeffrey Hallock. "Frequently Requested Statistics on Immigrants and Immigration in the United States." *Migration Policy Institute*. MPI, 8 Feb. 2018. Web. 6 Apr. 2018.

3. Kristen Bahler. "Unemployment Is Really Low. So Why Can't These People Find Jobs?" *Time*. Time, 22 May 2017. Web. 5 Dec. 2017.

4. Laura Bliss. "Rent Is Affordable to Low-Wage Workers in Exactly 12 US Counties." *CityLab*. CityLab, 9 June 2017. Web. 6 Mar. 2018.

5. "History of Federal Minimum Wage." *US Department of Labor*. USDL, n.d. Web. 5 Dec. 2017.

6. Grace Donnelly. "The Minimum Wage Will Increase on January 1 for 18 States and 20 Cities." *Fortune*. Fortune, 20 Dec. 2017. Web. 14 Mar. 2018.

7. "The Effects of a Minimum-Wage Increase on Employment and Family Income." *Congressional Budget Office*. CBO, n.d. Web. 5 Dec. 2017.

8. Robert Rector. "Understanding Poverty in America." *National Review*. National Review, 10 Sept. 2009. Web. 5 Dec. 2017.

9. Kathryn Edin and H. Luke Schaefer. *$2.00 Per Day: Living on Almost Nothing in America*. Boston: Houghton Mifflin, 2015. Print. xvii.

10. "Poverty by Race/Ethnicity." *Kaiser Family Foundation*. KFF, n.d. Web. 6 Dec. 2017.

11. "Household Incomes: The Value of Higher Education." *AdvisorPerspectives.com*. Advisor Perspectives, n.d. Web. 5 Dec. 2017.

12. "Digest of Education Statistics, Table 219.75." *National Center for Education Statistics*. NCES, Nov. 2016. Web. 6 Apr. 2018.

13. "Indicators of Higher Education Equity in the United States." *Pell Institute*. Pell Institute, 2018. Web. 6 Apr. 2018.

14. Kimberly Amadeo. "What Is Average Income in the USA? Family, Household, History." *TheBalance.com*. The Balance, 9 Mar. 2018. Web. 6 Apr. 2018.

15. Lydia DePillis. "America's Wealth Gap." *CNN Money*. CNN, 3 Nov. 2017. Web. 5 Dec. 2017.

16. Elias Isquith. "We're Facing a Vicious Cycle." *Salon*. Salon, 17 Feb. 2015. Web. 5 Dec. 2017.

CHAPTER 3. AMERICA'S WAR ON POVERTY

1. Michael Harrington. *The Other America: Poverty in the United States*. New York: Simon, 1981. Print. 2.

2. Harrington, *The Other America*, 3–4.

3. "Lyndon B. Johnson: Annual Message to the Congress on the State of the Union." *American Presidency Project*. American Presidency Project, 8 Jan. 1964. Web. 14 Dec. 2017.

4. "Lyndon B. Johnson: Remarks at the University of Michigan." *American Presidency Project*. American Presidency Project, 22 May 1964. Web. 14 Dec. 2017.

CHAPTER 4. URBAN POVERTY

1. "The World's Cities in 2016." United Nations. *United Nations*, n.d. Web. 6 Dec. 2017.

2. "US Cities Are Home to 62.7 Percent of the US Population." *Census Bureau*. USCB, 4 Mar. 2015. Web. 6 Dec. 2017.

3. Alan Berube and Cecile Murray. "Three Charts Showing You Poverty in US Cities and Metro Areas." *Brookings*. Brookings, 14 Sept. 2017. Web. 6 Dec. 2017.

4. Julie Mack. "See Richest, Poorest US Cities and Counties Based on New Census Data." *Michigan Live*. Michigan Live, 20 Sept. 2017. Web. 6 Mar 2018.

5. Wilmot Allen. "Urban Poverty in America: The Truly Disadvantaged Revisited." *Huffington Post*. Huffington Post, 25 Aug. 2014. Web. 6 Apr. 2018.

6. Dahleen Glanton. "Growing Up with Poverty and Violence: A North Lawndale Teen's Story." *Chicago Tribune*. Chicago Tribune, 10 Mar. 2017. Web. 6 Dec. 2017.

7. "The Gap: A Shortage of Affordable Homes." *National Low Income Housing Coalition*. NLIHC, Mar. 2017. Web. 6 Dec. 2017.

8. "Long-Term Welfare Recipients Found Overwhelmingly Concentrated in Urban Areas." *Brookings*. Brookings, 25 Sept. 2002. Web. 6 Dec. 2017.

9. Maya Miller. "Report: Impoverished Households Face 'Critical' Rental Shortage." *Chicago Tonight*. Chicago Tribune, 6 Mar. 2017. Web. 6 Dec. 2017.

10. "Cost of Living." *CNN Money*. CNN, n.d. Web. 22 Jan. 2018.

11. William Frey. "White Neighborhoods Get Modestly More Diverse." *Brookings*. Brookings, 13 Dec. 2016. Web. 6 Dec. 2017.

12. "A Profile of the Working Poor, 2015." *Bureau of Labor Statistics*. BLS, Apr. 2017. Web. 6 Dec. 2017.

13. David K Shipler. *The Working Poor: Invisible in America*. New York: Vintage, 2005. Print. 4.

14. Dan Kopf. "American Poverty Is Moving to the Suburbs." *Quartz Media*. Quartz, 9 June 2017. Web. 6 Dec. 2017.

15. Elizabeth Kneebone. "The Changing Geography of U.S. Poverty." *Brookings*. Brookings, 15 Feb. 2017. Web. 6 Dec. 2017.

16. Steve Hargreaves. "America's Jobs Are Moving to the Suburbs." *CNN Money*. CNN, 18 Apr. 2013. Web. 6 Dec. 2017.

17. Ed Leefeldt. "Minorities Move to the Suburbs and So Does Poverty." *Moneywatch*. CBS News, 4 Oct. 2016. Web, 6 Dec. 2017.

CHAPTER 5. POVERTY IN RURAL AMERICA

1. Andria Caruthers. "Mapping Poverty in the Appalachian Region." *Community Commons*. Community Commons, 9 Aug. 2016. Web. 7 Dec. 2017.

2. Scott Rodd. "This Is What Poverty Looks Like." *ThinkProgress*. ThinkProgress, 11 Mar. 2015. Web. 7 Dec. 2017.

3. Rodd, "This Is What Poverty Looks Like."

4. Alemayehu Bishaw and Craig Benson. "Poverty: 2015 and 2016." *Census Bureau*. USCB, n.d. Web. 7 Dec. 2017.

5. Scott Rodd. "The Depths of Poverty in the Deep South." *ThinkProgress*. ThinkProgress, 15 June 2015. Web. 7 Dec. 2017.

SOURCE NOTES
CONTINUED

6. "Decades Go By Yet Child Hunger and Poverty Endure in the Delta." *University of Mississippi Medical Center*. University of Mississippi, n.d. Web. 2017.

7. Emrys Eller. "Fighting Hunger in the Mississippi Delta." *Hechinger Report*. Hechinger Report, 17 Aug. 2017. Web. 7 Dec. 2017.

8. Della Hasselle. "Mississippi's Lost Babies." *Al Jazeera*. Al Jazeera, 17 Dec. 2015. Web. 7 Dec. 2017.

9. Justin Fox. "How Mississippi Is Worse Off Than Bangladesh." *Bloomberg View*. Bloomberg, 14 Mar. 2017. Web. 7 Dec. 2017.

10. Daniel Uribe. "2015 RGV Demographics." *Workforce Solutions*. Workforce Solutions, 22 Apr. 2015. Web. 7 Dec. 2017.

11. Alexa Ura. "Latest Census Data Shows Poverty Rate Highest at Border, Lowest in Suburbs." *Texas Tribune*. Texas Tribune, 19 Jan. 2016. Web. 7 Dec. 2017.

12. "Child Poverty." *USDA Economic Research Service*. USDA, 25 Oct. 2017. Web. 6 Mar. 2018.

13. Patrick Strickland. "Living on the Edges: Life in the Colonias of Texas." *Al Jazeera*. Al Jazeera, 5 Nov. 2016. Web. 7 Dec. 2017.

14. Trymaine Lee. "Dark Valley: Life in the Shadows." *MSNBC*. MSNBC, n.d. Web. 7 Dec. 2017.

15. "Disability Characteristics." *Census Bureau*. USCB, n.d. Web. 7 Dec. 2017.

16. Cynthia M. Duncan. *Worlds Apart*. New Haven, CT: Yale UP, 1999. Print. 45-47.

17. Terrence McCoy. "Disabled, or Just Desperate? Rural Americans Turn to Disability as Jobs Dry Up." *Washington Post*. Washington Post, 30 Mar. 2017. Web. 7 Dec. 2017.

18. Valerie Wilson and Zane Mokhiber. "2016 ACS Shows Stubbornly High Native American Poverty." *Economic Policy Institute*. Economic Policy Institute, 15 Sept. 2017. Web. 7 Dec. 2017.

19. "Labor Force Characteristics by Race and Ethnicity, 2015." *Bureau of Labor Statistics*. BLS, n.d. Web. 7 Dec. 2017.

20. Shawn Regan. "5 Ways the Government Keeps Native Americans in Poverty." *Forbes*. Forbes, 13 Mar. 2014. Web. 7 Dec. 2017.

CHAPTER 6. HOMELESSNESS

1. "The Rise of Homelessness in the 1980s." *KCET*. KCET, 22 Feb. 2017. Web. 11 Dec. 2017.

2. Martha R. Burt. "Causes of the Growth of Homelessness During the 1980s." *Housing Policy Debate*. Housing Policy Debate, n.d. Web. 11 Dec. 2017.

3. "The State of Homelessness in America." *National Alliance to End Homelessness*. NAEH, n.d. Web. 2017.

4. "The 2016 Annual Homeless Assessment Report (AHAR) to Congress." *US Department of Housing and Urban Development*. HUD, Nov. 2016. Web. 11 Dec. 2017.

5. "The 15 Most Homeless Cities in the World." *TheRichest*. TheRichest, n.d. Web. 11 Dec. 2017.

6. "Children and Families." *National Alliance to End Homelessness*. NAEH, n.d. Web. 22 Jan. 2018.

7. "Interview with Ronald Frankford." *International Brotherhood of Veterans*. IBV, 11 July 2015. Web. 11 Dec. 2017.

8. "Interview with Ronald Frankford."

9. "Youth Homelessness." *National Coalition for the Homeless*. NCH, n.d. Web. 11 Dec. 2017.

10. "Youth and Young Adults." *National Alliance to End Homelessness*, NAEH, n.d. Web. 11 Dec. 2017.

11. "Why Some Homeless Choose the Streets over Shelters." *Talk of the Nation*. NPR, 6 Dec. 2012. Web. 11 Dec. 2015.

12. "Why Are People Homeless?" *National Coalition for the Homeless*. NCH, n.d. Web. 11 Dec. 2017.

CHAPTER 7. HEALTH, HEALTH CARE, AND POVERTY

1. Mark Robert Rank. *One Nation, Underprivileged.* New York: Oxford UP, 2004. Print. 39.

2. Raj Chetty, et al. "The Association Between Income and Life Expectancy in the United States, 2001-2014." *Journal of the American Medical Association.* 315.16 (Jan. 2016): 1750–1966.

3. "Serious Mental Illness Among Adults Below the Poverty Line." *Substance Abuse and Mental Health Administration.* CBHSQ Report, November 2016. Web. 12 Dec. 2017.

4. Lisa Esposito. "The Countless Ways Poverty Affects People's Health." *US News and World Report.* US News and World Report, 20 Apr. 2016. Web. 12 Dec. 2017.

5. Esposito, "The Countless Ways Poverty Affects People's Health."

6. Karen Seccombe. *Families in Poverty.* New York: Ally and Bacon, 2007. Print. 57.

7. "Economic Security for Seniors Facts." *National Coalition on Aging.* NCA, n.d. Web. 2017.

8. "Health Care on a Budget." *Kaiser Family Foundation.* Kaiser, n.d. Web. 12 Dec. 2017.

9. "Fact Sheet." *Social Security Administration.* SSA, n.d. Web. 12 Dec. 2017.

10. Adam Nagourney. "Old and on the Street: The Graying of America's Homeless." *New York Times.* New York Times, 31 May 2016. Web. 23 Mar. 2018.

11. "Lead Poisoning." *KidsHealth.org.* KidsHealth, n.d. Web. 12 Dec. 2017.

12. Esposito, "The Countless Ways Poverty Affects People's Health."

13. "Poor and in Poor Health." *Institute for Research on Poverty.* U of Wisconsin, n.d. Web. 12 Dec. 2017.

14. Allen, Heidi, et al. "The Role of Stigma in Access to Health Care for the Poor." *Milbank Quarterly* 92.2 (June 2014): 289–318.

15. Alvin Powell. "Cost of Inequality." *Harvard Gazette.* Harvard, 22 Feb. 2016. Web. 12 Dec. 2017.

CHAPTER 8. EDUCATION AND POVERTY

1. "Starting School at a Disadvantage." Brookings. *Brookings*, Mar. 2012. Web. 13 Dec. 2017.

2. "School Poverty: United States." *National Equity Atlas.* NEA, n.d. Web. 13 Dec. 2017.

3. Alana Semuels. "Good School, Rich School; Bad School, Poor School." *Atlantic.* Atlantic, 25 Aug. 2016. Web. 22 Jan. 2018.

4. Janie Boschma and Ronald Brownstein. "The Concentration of Poverty in American Schools." *Atlantic.* Atlantic, 29 Feb. 2016. Web. 13 Dec. 2017.

5. Boschma and Brownstein, "The Concentration of Poverty in American Schools."

6. Todd Williams. "Poverty Is Not Destiny." *Dallas News.* Dallas News, Jan. 2015. Web. 6 Apr. 2018.

7. "Low Income Students Now a Majority in the Nation's Public Schools." *Southern Education Foundation.* Southern Education Foundation, 2018. Web. 6 Mar. 2018.

8. "National Survey of American Teachers." *Communities in Schools.* CiS, n.d. Web. 13 Dec. 2017.

9. "National Survey of American Teachers."

10. Lauren Camera. "Fewer Students Dropping Out of High School." *US News.* US News, 10 Nov. 2015. Web. 13 Dec. 2017.

11. "History of Head Start." *Office of Head Start.* Head Start, n.d. Web. 13 Dec. 2017.

CHAPTER 9. FIGHTING POVERTY TODAY

1. Marisa Schultz. "Trump Wants to Impose Work Requirement for Food Stamp Users." *New York Post.* New York Post, 22 May 2017. Web. 26 Jan. 2018.

2. Rachel Garfield and Robin Rudowitz. "Understanding the Intersection of Medicaid and Work." *Kaiser Family Foundation.* Kaiser, 7 Dec. 2017. Web. 26 Jan. 2018.

3. "Income and Poverty in the United States: 2014." *Census Bureau.* USCB, n.d. Web. 14 Dec. 2017.

4. Muhammad Yunus. *Creating a World Without Poverty.* New York: Public Affairs, 2008. Print 223.

INDEX

ABOUT THE
AUTHORS

DUCHESS HARRIS, JD, PHD

Professor Harris is the chair of the American Studies department at Macalester College and curator of the Duchess Harris Collection of ABDO books. She is the author and coauthor of recently released ABDO books including *Hidden Human Computers: The Black Women of NASA*, *Black Lives Matter*, and *Race and Policing*.

Before working with ABDO, she authored several other books on the topics of race, culture, and American history. She served as an associate editor for *Litigation News*, the American Bar Association Section of Litigation's quarterly flagship publication, and was the first editor in chief of *Law Raza*, an interactive online journal covering race and the law, published at William Mitchell College of Law. She has earned a PhD in American Studies from the University of Minnesota and a JD from William Mitchell College of Law.

NEL YOMTOV

Nel Yomtov is an award-winning author of nonfiction books and graphic novels for young readers. His writing passions include history, geography, military, nature, sports, biographies, and careers. Yomtov has also written, edited, and colored hundreds of Marvel comic books. Yomtov has served as editorial director of a children's nonfiction book publisher and as executive editor of Hammond World Atlas book division. Yomtov lives in the New York City area with his wife.